The Alice Effect

Diving Down the Rabbit Hole
of Your Dreams

by Megan Patiry

Printed in the United States of America

First Printing, 2021

ISBN 978-1-949321-29-6

All writings within this book belong to the author.

Cover Design by: Megan Patiry

A.B.Baird Publishing

66548 Highway 203

La Grande OR, 97850

USA

www.abbairdpublishing.com

To Mom,

who's simple idea to go to the library together

charted my destiny.

Table of Contents

"'The time has come, 'the walrus said
'to talk of many things:
Of shoes - and ships - and sealing wax
- Of cabbages and Kings -
And why the sea is boiling hot
And whether pigs have wings.'"

- Alice in Wonderland, Lewis Carroll

<u>Conclusion</u>

When I ask you, "Have you ever read a book backwards, from the last chapter to the first?" I know what you are likely thinking: "Why on Earth would I do that? I'd obviously spoil the ending!"

And I'd answer, "Perhaps. But what if you gained the power to predict beginnings?"

To put that question into perspective (and to why I'm asking such a strange question), we can tip our heads over to the East.

In Mandarin Chinese, the idea of time is expressed very differently than in the English language. In fact, one might say it's backwards. This is because the Mandarin conceptualization of time is expressed in a different order. Unlike in languages such as English, which see the future as "ahead" (i.e.: "We look forward to a bright future.") and the past as "behind" (i.e.: "All of the things we left behind."), Mandarin sees the future and the past from a different perspective. [1] So different, in fact, that if we were to write or speak in Mandarin, we would put the past character in front of the future character, as if the past were coming after the future.

Future —> Past

Because we are so accustomed to the past being "behind" us and the future being "ahead," this concept seems intensely confusing. Why would the past come after the future, if it has already gone? And, what does this have to do with creativity or new beginnings?

This is where the metaphorical and philosophical implications of putting the past after the future comes in to answer these questions. Studies are now showing that the language we speak creates "space-time mappings" in our brains that affect how we view the world, and thus how we interact in it.

In English, the past has gone. Today is a new day, so we tend to not put much emphasis on what happened "before." In Mandarin, however, one might tend to "see" the past as a foundation or stepping stone to the future, which is why the character is "in front," while seeing the future as what comes "behind" it.

So, just by looking at the structure of Mandarin, we can see that what we have done in the past acts as the foundation of our future … and that in order to predict that future, all we have to do is turn our gaze toward our past.

Now, this is not meant to say that you are defined by your past - quite the opposite! It simply means that in the next few seconds, this sentence that you are reading now will be a part of your past, as the past is being created in every moment. And, every moment is simultaneously being influenced by your own perspectives and filters that you have gathered throughout your past. So theoretically, if we looked at your past and what you learned there, we can make an educated guess as what kind of future you are creating.

How is this relevant to the idea of reading a book from the Conclusion to the Beginning?

Because we have to look at our past (the conclusion) in order to be able to change our future (the beginning, or Now).

Yes, it is true that tomorrow is a new day ... but it is equally as true that tomorrow is defined by the perspectives, preconceived notions, and biases that we continue to carry with us from our past. By going back to our past and unearthing these stones, we can open ourselves to new space-time mappings of the world. We can begin to perceive differently, which can turn our world upside down in the best of ways.

I also wanted to shake you out of the routine of accepting things the way they have "always been" in your personal experience, so that you can begin to think of the way they could be, with just a little creativity. After all, now you know that just by switching up the way we write and structure our own language, we can radically change the way we see everything. This change in viewpoint has always been the master key to innovation, and will now act as your master key to your new idea (and new life).

When the idea came to me for this book, I sat down to begin and the thought popped into my head, "Why do we label the end of a book The End, when in fact, if a book is meant to alter our lives in some way, it should actually be 'The Beginning'?" After I put a book down, I should be beginning, or at least contemplating, something new, yes?

Some change should (ideally) be made, either in the physical or in my mindset. I should, at the very least, have a lightbulb moment that sparks some kind of new light to shine out across the sea of my consciousness, which might stimulate an internal shift (a beginning).

I wanted to bring to your awareness that even the nonchalant act of accepting the "way things are" when it comes to something as simple book structure, means that we are likely accepting many other things at face value, and missing unique opportunities to create something new at every turn.

Here, I want you to experience something different. To read the last chapter of this book and feel like a door has opened in your life. A door to a realm where all things were possible - one that you lost your directions to as a child, because someone told you it did not exist.

We will start with where you are now, an adult (an "End" result, if you will) with quite a bit of past to look at ... and we will move toward your

Future. We'll look at how your childhood shaped the lens out of which you see the world, and how this lens was further altered and shrouded with preconceptions as you grew older that now severely limit your creativity, ability to innovate and generate ideas, and, frankly, your ability to excel beyond your wildest dreams. By returning to your beginning (your past) as a child, before you were indoctrinated with societal concepts and "the way things are," you will be able to tap into what I call The Alice Effect: a mindset that is without bias-infused filters, so you can truly see the world and all of its opportunities available directly in front of you.

We will also (and this is important) go through how you can keep the door to your new realm open and innovate with a childlike mindset, while integrating your new ideas into societal structure as a high-functioning adult ... because, well, that's where the true magic of turning your ideas into a life happens.

In other words:

> Here, you are going to innovate.
>
> *Why?*
>
> Because you have a blank slate.
>
> *Where on this new ocean will you go?*
>
> Toward that island, where geniuses grow.
>
> *And how will you know? How will you know the soil where this future will be sowed?*
>
> There! There it will whisper deep in your soul:
>
> > "I've known you
> > since the day I was born."

Chapter Five

The Setting Down of Stones

"If you have built castles in the air, your work need not be lost; there is where they should be. Now put foundations under them". - *Henry David Thoreau*

Have you ever noticed that as you have gotten older, the amount of "stuff" you have accumulated has exponentially increased alongside your age?

I remember when having nothing but a pacifier and a mother to my name was enough to make me smile giddily at strangers and be completely content in the world. (Well, I actually don't remember this at all, but from observing plenty of infants throughout my life, I'm going to take a wild guess that this early happiness was the case for myself as well.)

I think back now, to those days I do fully remember, like when I was without a cell phone or access to the internet, and wonder: "What happened? Where did that aliveness go? That feeling that anything was possible, and that there was something magical hidden behind everything I encountered? When did I stop asking 'Why? 'when I was presented with 'common 'or 'popular ' things? Where am I, now? Who have I become?"

And I have realized that the reality is that none of us experiencing this feeling have become someone else, or lost our ability to dream, to be in awe of life, and to be tuned to possibility ... but that we're simply carrying too much.

We start out life with an open sack, if you will (you can also think of this as an open mind and open heart). As we get older, we begin to stuff this sack with all of the things we have learned. Some of these things were good, especially if we were raised by parents who encouraged us to think outside of the box and ask a lot of questions; however, many of these things were simply ideas proposed by others of "how things are" in society and in the world and Universe at large.

To use a big example, in the time of Galileo Galilei, "the way things were" was that the Sun revolved around the Earth, as dictated by religious leaders. In households, at the time, children were raised being told by their parents, "this is the way it is."

Then, Galileo came along and decided, "You know what? I'm going to look at the sky differently." (This is obviously not a direct quote, but you get the gist). He decided to question the assumption everyone (society) was making that the Sun revolved around the Earth, and asked, "What if?" instead.

And now, thanks to Galileo's ability to set down his sack of societal programming and "the way things are," we now know that the Earth indeed revolves around the Sun! In fact, we now have an entire concept of how the solar system looks and operates thanks to one man's ability to let go of everything he "knew."

Another big, modern example of what happens when we set down our sack of preconceived notions begins with, ironically, the idea of packing our bags.

Pre-2008, when you travelled, you stayed in a hotel. It was just the "way things were," and there really were no other options. But, as we now know, there is a gigantic alternative to staying in a hotel when travelling, called: Airbnb.

The founders of Airbnb obviously knew the "way things were" when they travelled, as I am sure they've had to book a hotel at least once in their lives. But again, their idea of "What if?" won out, and allowed them to unpack their bags of preconceived notions … in someone else's home for the night!

Here, we see that by removing the idea of "You stay in a hotel when you travel" from the sack of preconceived notions, a new, extremely successful idea was able to come to light.

Here we learn that to get to "What If?" we must let go of our attachment to "What has been."

Now, this does not mean we totally disregard what has been in the past (because remember, it shapes the future and is therefore good to glance at from time to time, as if we were writing in Mandarin), it's that we drop our attachment to "how it has always been."

Before dishwashers arrived on the scene, dishes were simply washed by hand … until someone questioned this and decided to ask, "What if something could do this for us? What if it does not have to be this way?" (overly dramatic for a question related to dish-washing, but alas …). The same concept goes for all major inventions, really, but it doesn't stop there. We can also see the same thing happening with great artists and artwork: for a time, a certain "style" of art will be the "norm" and most well-liked … until an artist comes along and says, "What if I did the strokes differently? What if I questioned what is considered 'art 'and created something entirely new?"

Take Pablo Picasso and Georges Braque, who revolutionized cubism in 1907, during an art age where extremely realistic and detailed still life paintings were "all the rage." Instead of attempting to fit their artistic talents into the box of what was trending, they removed the preconceived notion of what was art from their sack, and created an entirely new form of art featuring abstract shapes.

Even in the financial realm today, we see this occurring with the rise of cryptocurrency. For hundreds of years, currency has always been something physical. Be it gold, silver or copper coins, or paper bills, "the way things are" when it comes to money has been one of the most deeply ingrained societal constructs we know. However, someone (we actually don't have a definitive answer as to who this someone is, as there is intense speculation over who the creators of blockchain technology and Bitcoin really are) asked the question: "What if currency went digital? What if it was no longer physical, but could still allow us the ability to purchase physical things?" From there, "digital coins" were created, or mined, and are now being used and invested into by top-level companies and brands around the world, such as Tesla and Target.

I've experienced what I call the "emptied sack" phenomenon accidentally on many occasions, but one stands out as an exceptional experience. A few years ago I visited my Canadian boyfriend in Canada for the first time. By this point, I was obviously aware that he was an entrepreneur who made a living by creating medicinal mushroom elixirs. I was also aware that he often "brewed" these elixirs in a commercial kitchen in Toronto, but because I am American and we were in a long-distance relationship, I had yet to actually witness him doing so.

On the afternoon that I arrived, he also had to be at the kitchen, so asked if I wanted to check out the process and try my hand at helping. I agreed, and we arrived at the kitchen.

Now, to preface I will say we both have health in common, I have drank a lot of tea in my life, and have an idea of specific materials that are commonly used in the health industry, such as nut milk bags (these are natural cotton or hemp bags that filter out bits of almonds or other nuts after they are ground up from being blended with water to create a "milk").

As we started the brewing process, I noticed that a massive amount of herbs, spices, and barks were being added to giant cauldron-like vats filled with water, and were being brought to a boil in order to "extract" their nutrients. After this process was over, it was time to separate the liquid from the loose herbs and spices and, well, let me tell you, this was one of the most annoying and patience-testing things I have ever experienced. We basically had to drain all of the liquid out through a small hole at the bottom (which kept getting clogged with herbs) and then scoop out the herbs from these giant vats after we bottled the liquid. Overall, this scraping and dealing with the herbs took hours, and about midway-through the process, I had the thought, "What if it didn't have to be this way?" (not dramatic this time, which you'd agree with me if you'd had to do it).

Earlier, when I had looked at the vats boiling like cauldrons for the first time and saw the water start to darken, I'd had the immediate, child-like thought: "These look like giant tea cups!" I didn't really say anything at the time and just dismissed it as a random thought, but after scraping the herbs out of those cauldrons for an ungodly length of time, I decided to revisit that "random" thought.

I mulled it over in my mind for a minute and, after hesitating to say anything out of wondering whether it was out of line to suggest to someone else a "better" way of doing things within their business, I finally decided to spill my idea to my boyfriend at the end of the night. I asked, "What if you just put the herb mix into giant nut milk bags and place them in the water to steep, like a tea bag? Then you could just lift out and dump out the bags afterwards, avoiding hours of dealing with cleaning out the cauldrons?"

To under-exaggerate, he looked at me as if I'd spontaneously sprouted wings and stated I was actually a half-human, half-angelic hybrid. At first I thought he might be angry due to the mild confusion in his eyes, but then he just shook his head and said, "Are you serious? I've been doing this for 5 years straight, and never once did I see that as a possibility."

Needless to say, the bags were ordered that night, hours were taken off production time, and his product was able to double in sales due to being able to increase production speed.

Interestingly, even though he was a bit shocked at how I "came up" with the idea, there wasn't really a miraculous or otherworldly inspiration behind it in the least: it was the simple fact that I had absolutely zero preconceived notions about the process of brewing these elixirs. I had never tried it before, and so my mental bag was "empty." Meanwhile, he had been doing things "the way they were" for years, and due to being so heavily involved in the process, he never had the space in his sack to look at his own process with brand new eyes.

Now to be clear, this is not his fault or anyone else's "fault" by any means, and this also isn't meant to insinuate that he doesn't come up with brilliant ideas himself on a regular basis (in fact, he's done the same thing for me in my career many times, because his eyes are "fresh" to my work). It's simply an illustration of how our notions of "the way things are" in our lives can inhibit our ability to innovate and create. While, on the flip side, approaching things with an "open sack," or with an open mind as if we're seeing something for the first time, we can begin to see potentials we may have missed when we are simply "doing things the way they have always been done."

Speaking of being able to "see" things with new eyes or an open sack, and to go back to language for a moment, a very interesting discovery in linguistics has shown that even our native language affects what we can and cannot see.

This is a huge discovery, because it basically states that we could be missing important things in our environment simply due to the words we are using or not using. Think of this as the equivalent of the entire world being the cauldron we are brewing loose herbs in, and because this is the only "language" we know, we never see a better way of steeping the herbs (aka: we never see an alternative way of doing something in our lives).

The idea that the language we speak influences how we conceptualize and experience the world is recognized as the Sapir-Whorf hypothesis, and in this study it was applied to color perception as a means to show how individuals whose native languages have different color categories don't see the world in the same way. [3]

In the study, Martin Maier and Rasha Abdel Rahman at the Humboldt University of Berlin illustrate that linguistic differences affect visual processing to the point of determining whether or not someone will see a colored shape or not. They write: "Our native language is thus one of the forces that determine what we consciously perceive."

The basis of the study shows how color categories vary between languages; for instance, in both Greek and Russian, there is a dedicated category word for "light blue" and "dark blue," but no specific word for "blue" as an overarching category. On the other hand, in German, there is just one word for "blue" (blau) to cover all the varying shades of blue.

Oddly, when it comes to the color green, Greek, Russian, and German each have an overarching category word to describe all shades of "green."

Other research has already shown that having specific category words for objects quickens our ability to identify those objects. For instance, native Russian speakers are able to distinguish between light blue and dark blue color patches faster than native English speakers, simply because they have more category words to describe shades of "blue."

This study takes this research a step further to show how language may influence whether we become conscious of something in our environment at all. In the trial, 28 native Greek-speakers were presented with 13 colored geometric shapes against a background of a different color. They were asked to pay attention to a grey semi-circle, which was there to pull at their attention during the experiment. They then presented the participants with a colored triangle in 80 percent of the trials, and asked whether the participants spotted it when it appeared.

This triangle was either light blue against a dark blue background, light green against a dark green circle, or light or dark blue against a light or dark green background circle. At the end of the trial, the participants were asked how much of the triangle they had seen, ranging from: not seeing anything at all, to seeing a slight impression of a triangle, to seeing a complete triangle.

It turns out the Greek speakers were more likely to see the triangle when it was light blue against dark blue, than when it was light green against dark green … simply because the Greek speakers have more category words or descriptions of the shades of the color "blue" than they do of "green"!

Interestingly, the same results were found with the native Russian speakers, who share the same color categories as the Greeks.

Now, while we can't do too much in regards to our native tongues, we can recognize that this has huge implications: the very things we are exposed to everyday (such as our native language) can limit our perception ... to the point that we may become blind to certain things, even though they are technically in our field of vision.

How does this happen? Again, we are carrying too many preconceived notions in our sacks. We are, essentially, walking around with a native language that has very, very few alternative category words for just about everything, making our options for what something "could be" very limited. Not to mention, these notions not only stuff our bags so full with "the way things are" that we don't have room for new perceptions, but they are also heavy. They weigh down our eyelids, making it difficult to "see" new ideas, opportunities for innovations, and alternative pathways to our dreams, while simultaneously draining us of the energy that comes from inspiration.

This is why it is crucial to practice setting down the stones inside your sack, even just temporarily. You may be used to their weight, it may feel uncomfortable to be without it, but I assure you: once you see the possibilities that pop up when you start to look at things with "new eyes," you'll be more than happy to, instead of carrying those stones on your back, use them as stepping stones to your future.

....

An Exercise for Unpacking Preconceived Notions:

The next time you look at something you see everyday, I want you to pause. Pause, and after your mind has labelled this object, I want you to pretend that you've never seen it before. I want you to imagine you are a child again, and that you have no knowledge of what you're looking at … but you are extremely curious to know what it is and how it works. But (and this is the hard part) I want you to avoid labeling what you are seeing at all. Leave your mind as open as possible to what you have just seen. This is a perception-primer for the follow-up exercise below.

Now, after you've tried the above a couple times throughout your day, I want you to come home and find a quiet space, light a candle, grab a piece of paper or a journal, and sink back into your child-self again. I want you to imagine a time when you were with one of your parents or grandparents, and they were telling you how something worked (perhaps it was a toy, something around the house, something to do with school, etc) a personal memory here is key, so take some time to think about a specific memory of being told "what something was" or "how something worked." Then, I want you to imagine that, instead of your parent being there to tell you how this object or process worked, that you are alone. If that seems scary for any reason, imagine they walked into the kitchen to take a phone call.

Now, I want you to look at the object. What do you think it is, just by looking at it? How do you think it works? Why do you think that?

Once you get a couple answers, I want you to set down that object, and come back to your adult self. Begin to imagine a specific object you've used every day as an adult: a car visor (that piece in your car above the steering wheel you pull down to shield your eyes from the sun). I want you to imagine that you are using it for the first time.

You are driving, and the sun is low on the horizon, so you flip down this thing called a visor. It works for a moment, but then the sun sets lower - too low to be blocked by the visor. And, even if the visor could be pulled down further, it would totally block your view. The sun is in your eyes, and you are, in essence, driving half-blind due to how the visor was created.

Pause here. With the image of the visor in hand, I want you to open your eyes, grab your journal, and answer these questions:

- How does the visor work?

- What material is the visor made out of?

- How could the visor work differently? (don't censor any ideas that pop up)

- What if the visor were made of a different material?

- What type of material could it be made out of instead?

- Is the visor similar to anything else?

- What stopped me from asking these questions about the visor in the past?

Now, look over your answers. What kind of new visor did you create?

I have news for you: if you imagined a clear or transparent visor (perhaps made out of a similar material to sunglasses), you just came up with the same invention as a wildly successful company that creates clear visors that replace "standard" visors in cars!

Just by pausing and dwelling on something that you have seen every single day while driving, and deciding to truly look at it instead of just assuming "this is just the way car visors are," then getting curious like a child about it, you were able to come up with quite the invention!

And the best part? That process you just did can be replicated again and again, in whatever field you're in.

This is the perfect illustration of how even seemingly "ultra-normal" objects can have hidden potentials lying within them just waiting for improvement. And notice: it could be the smallest of "improvements" that could change not only your life, but thousands of others 'lives if you turn your idea into a product.

Again, when we look at innovations like these from the outside, it's easy to feel a sort of awe at how someone could come up with such an amazing idea ... but this feeling is a trap. Now, this isn't to say that we can't admire someone else's mind or idea, as they truly are admirable, but to be awestruck at another's ability to innovate or create is a trap for your own abilities, simply because the ability to create and innovate rests within every single one of us. It is not reserved for "geniuses" or "lucky" souls or people who were raised by creative parents. It isn't reserved for PhDs, specific races, specific genders, or specific countries.

It's reserved for those who have emptied their sacks, so that inspiration can flood in, water the walls, plant new soil, and encourage the growth of new ideas. It's for those that can set down their stones of notions and biases of "how things are" and can start asking more and more often: "What if?"

<u>Chapter Four</u>

Becoming the Sponge

"Then why do you want to know?

Because learning does not consist only of knowing
what we must or we can do,
but also of knowing what we could do." - *Umberto
Eco*

You've probably heard this saying about children: "They're like little sponges!"

Everything a child sees, he or she is curious about, wanting to touch it, taste it, smell it, play with it, eat it, you name it (oh, and they will want to name it).

Why are they so curious and so primed to absorb knowledge?

Because their life sacks are empty, waiting to be filled with new information.

If you were to refrain from telling a child how something worked, they would tinker with it until they, at the very least, figured out how to do something with it, even if it wasn't the "correct" usage according to us adults, simply because they are stimulated by curiosity.

One Fall, I went out pine cone-picking in the forest nearby with a few of my step-nieces. Each of us had our own plastic bags to stuff with pinecones (the irony of stuffing bags, I know) and in just an hour or so, the bags were getting heavier.

One of my step-nieces in particular was tired of carrying her bag (I believe she was 5 or 6 at the time) and I saw her constantly shifting it around. I didn't really say or think anything of it, as all of our bags were getting heavy on our arms.

A few minutes later, I turned around and saw her rearranging the bag across a clearing … and the next thing I knew, she had put her tiny arms through the loops of the plastic bag behind her, and it suddenly became a makeshift backpack. I remember laughing and saying, "Wow! Good idea. How did you do that?" And she simply looked at me and said it was like how her mom put on her coat!

Now, maybe she has used a backpack before, or saw someone else use one, but the point remains: children are overflowing with creativity, and if you leave them to their own devices (within reason) they will often surprise you with their "inventions."

Curiosity plays a key role in this abundance of creativity. Because children genuinely want to know how something works (but have no preconceived notion of it) they are inspired to find a way to make it work. They desire to soak up any and all kinds of knowledge, even if it's knowledge they have gained through their own games and experiments.

One of the things we tend to lose as adults is this desire to learn, and to be more specific, this deep curiosity regarding all types of things. The goal in the earlier chapter was not to empty your sack and leave it empty forever - it was to simply empty it of everything you have been conditioned to believe as "true," so you can start seeing possibility like a child again. After you have let go of the heavy stones of bias, you can begin to get curious again. To become sponge-like as you look at the world. Gathering in data from all types of places, without the filters of programming or conditioning to stop you from truly seeing. Like in the earlier study where native speakers saw more colored geometric shapes because they had more category words for colors, you want to sponge up as many "category words" for everything, so that you can see more possibility in front of you at all times.

An easy way to "become the sponge" is to become the watcher of your own thoughts and reactions. If you have done any form of meditation, you are probably familiar with the concept of watching your "monkey mind" jump across the trees of thoughts in your brain, while remaining the observer who is continually focused on your breath.

Who is that observer of the monkey? The True You.

When you have a thought, then become simultaneously aware that you are having a thought, something interesting happens. You can begin to catch your own preconceived notions as they arise.

Take, for example, what is around me at the exact moment I'm writing this. I'm in my living room, and I've just looked up from my computer and over at two decorative vases sitting on the end table. My mind recognized these as "vases," but since I have made a habit of being able to observe and question my own thoughts, I immediately correct this "observation" and ask, "Are they really just vases? Could they be something else?" In just a few moments, I have concluded they could also be used as tealight holders (because they are slightly clear and have an open top), large candles themselves (if I poured wax into them), and even as plant pots (probably just succulents though, because there are no drainage holes).

If I wanted to, I could get similar "vases" to these, which were designed simply to be a decoration in and of themselves, and sell them as candles or candle holders online or at a local market, possibly even with my own branding on them (if I get them through a wholesaler)! From this thought process alone, I could become an entrepreneur who now sells these "vases" as something else.

A similar phenomenon actually occurred a few years ago with the Mason jar craze. I'm not sure who the first "genius" was that made candles out of Mason jars, or began selling single-serving food products like yogurt packaged in Mason jars, but wow - what an out-of-the-box idea to use an old jar for something different than what was intended! And as we know, this simple idea spread like wildfire across the world.

If you can begin to watch your thoughts and notice when you label something, then ask "Could it be different? How?" ... you effectively become a sponge. Why? Because you have gone from preconceived notion to curious, and thus are primed for new information.

Mind you, the process of setting down your sack of stones and becoming the sponge can be used across all disciplines. We can see examples of it in yoga, for instance. Bikram yoga, as you may have heard before, is a specific sequence of yoga poses ... but there is one important, unique addition: the room where one practices Bikram is heated.

Now, I'm not going to assume to know Bikram's thought process when he developed the Bikram method, but it is self-evident to look at "yoga" and see that, just maybe, Bikram asked, "What could make yoga different? What if I added something else that was healthy to it?" (which, sweating is considered extremely healthy, especially for detoxification).

Alas, we are left with Bikram yoga, which has also spread across the globe.

Side note on this, so you can also hear a personal example of this: I've had many discussions with a dear friend of mine that were stimulated by yoga and yoga mats. We both observed how Bikram added heat to yoga, so we talked about how we could possibly add something to yoga as well, and if so, what would it be? (By the way, I'm going to just throw these ideas out to you, because I truly believe ideas are limitless once we begin to train our minds to see them. We haven't done anything with the ideas themselves, so feel free to elaborate on them and use them!)

We decided that a few cool ideas would be to either: 1. Design yoga mats that were simultaneously acupressure mats, but with smaller pressure points due to all of the movement; and 2. Embed various types of crystals into the edges of the mats in a decorative way, but with flat tops for safety. For yin yoga, which is more gentle and slow, we could use "gentle" stones that generate a peaceful energy, such as rose quartz or lapis lazuli, and for more intense yoga sequences, like Ashtanga, we could use stimulating stones like bloodstone.

We ended up getting further than this, but this just goes to show that when you train your mind to remain open and sponge-like, you can see so much more than what is in front of you.

We can even go to a higher level in the sciences and see how becoming the sponge for new ideas is occurring now. If you are familiar with quantum physics, you'll know that quantum particles are smaller than atoms ... which were once declared "the smallest particles in existence."

We now know that in fact, there are smaller particles even than protons and neutrons, which make up atoms, and these are called quarks.

This discovery could have easily arisen from a physicist (well, anyone really) asking a simple question, "What if the atom is not the smallest particle? What if there are smaller things than even a proton?"

What is within these two questions? Dropping the preconceived notion of "this is the way it is," and turning the mind into a sponge for new input after asking, "What if?"

Another key practice for becoming the sponge is not only being ready to soak up information at any given time, but to actively seek out information from various sources. We will get into this deeper in the following chapters, but in essence, feeding your mind with new ideas and new concepts is going to radically improve your ability to generate ideas and "see" possibilities in everything. This is similar to the color category idea: the more category words (information) you have available, the more "colors" (possibilities) you can see. This may seem to directly contradict the idea of emptying your sack (after all, aren't we supposed to be getting rid of information, not stuffing it in?), but these ideas are vastly different due to the state of the mind, or mind-state, they occur in.

When our sack is full before we consciously decide to empty it and set down our stones of preconceived notions, we are essentially full of biases, whether they are ours or other individuals'.

When we become the sponge, we are sponging up new information and new ideas, and since we can now recognize preconceived notions and biases, we can take in this information without becoming attached to it. And, when we are not attached to new information, we can reference it without being blinded by it ... which allows us to begin the process of truly seeing.

Speaking of information, did you know that our brains have been described as the largest quantum computers in existence, with the ability to store roughly 2.5 million gigabytes of digital memory? [4]

Before I elaborate, I want to make sure you paused after reading that statement, and asked, "What if it wasn't the largest quantum computer? What if data was also stored somewhere else?" because you would then discover after a small amount of research, that extremely large amounts of data are also stored elsewhere: in your DNA!

In fact, DNA could store the entirety of the world's data … in just one room. [5] Now, this data may or may not be digital memory, but it is data, and by simply questioning a statement, do you see how we can arrive at very valuable new information? Can you see how if you asked the right question just once, and became the sponge, you might make an extremely important discovery?

At the end of everyday, you cannot fear going down the rabbit hole with information, no matter what that information is or who the source of the information is. Everything is up for grabs to question and consider, and while you may question something and not get a different answer (aka: the thing your questioning really is "how it is"), the act of questioning itself is rewiring your brain for enhanced curiosity and heightened observance. Not every question regarding every preconceived notion is going to lead to a different notion ... but it will lead to a mindstate that will be as valuable as gold.

....

<u>An Exercise to Become the Sponge</u>

For this exercise, I want you to consider the eyelashes.

As I'm writing this, I'm sitting in a loud cafe in San Francisco, Mexico (that's right, it even has its own Golden Gate bridge, which stretches in a rainbow of tourist-attracting colors over a small drainage river-system), and frankly, I'm annoyed.

I'm annoyed because I really don't enjoy or work well in noise … but I also don't do either of those things well without Wi-Fi either. So here I am.

Blenders blending smoothies are blaring. The birds have begun a symphony of bellowing. The cars are creaking onto the surface of the roads, like giant Krakens breaking the surface of the sea.

In the middle of all of this, people are trying to talk over everything, making this moment the last one I want to "become the sponge" in. In truth, I want to put my headphones in and blinders on and drown out the world so I can work.

However, the moment before I do just that, I hear a voice spring up and out from the ocean of sounds:

> "I heard once that true awareness is also the ability to see your eyelashes. We tend to see everything so far away from us, that we forget to see things that are literally in front of our eyes."

After I heard this, I started laughing, because becoming the sponge also involves the ability to see your eyelashes! In this moment in the cafe, I assumed there would be nothing in this environment I would learn anything from, and so I was tempted to not become the sponge, or be open to an experience/lesson/idea sitting right in front of me.

So for this exercise and from here on out, I want you to have a simple goal: to learn something new everyday, and to be open to learning anything new, even in familiar environments.

Whether you pick up a new book (fiction or nonfiction), take a class of some sort, talk to a stranger in a familiar cafe - anything you can do that is new and opens you to new experiences, I want you to do it. And, while this new thing is occurring, I want you to become the sponge. Drop every preconceived idea you have about what you are doing and just observe and ask questions. Better yet, ask the questions that were listed in the following exercise, but apply it to a new thing you learned.

Chapter Three

The Question for Every Answer

"It is not that I am so smart. But I stay with the questions much longer." - *Einstein*

Did you know that there is a question for every answer?

I know. The obviousness is astounding.

However, it seems that even though we know this to be true, we've stopped asking the amount of obvious questions we did when we were younger. Why is this?

One word: programming.

Once we reach a certain age, reactions to our questioning of the systems of adulthood tend to get a bit more harsh. I remember clearly asking my mum one day after coming home from elementary school (probably the 3rd or 4th grade): "Why do I have to spend as much time in music class as I do art class?" As a child who was pretty gifted in art (enough to have pieces in a local museum in Florida by the time I reached 5th grade), the idea that I was not "allowed" to be taught more of something I was good at and interested in (versus music, which I was neutral toward) was disturbing to me.

Of course, my mum obviously didn't want to launch into explaining the details of the school system, why it was the way it was, how it came to be, and why I couldn't change it, etc … and so she told me that it was just because "that's the why school is."

I remember promptly looking for alternatives to "the way it was" and asked one of my teachers if it was possible if I could "learn from home." She seemed surprised, but of course informed me that I could be "home-schooled."

Of course, this was the greatest news ever at the time! If no teachers were there to watch how much time I spent doing my art or music lessons, and if I could squeeze my music lessons into a shorter time frame than my physical "class" in school required me to be there, well then I could spend more time learning about art!

It seemed like a win to me. So when I got home that day, I eagerly told my mom I wanted to be homeschooled. "Wouldn't it be great?" I'd said. "You wouldn't have to drive me to school anymore or pack my lunch (a fine persuasion tactic for a parent, if I don't say so myself), and I could do more art!"

What I failed to realize at the time was that being a single mum was not as easy as sitting home all day homeschooling your child, as much as I could tell she wanted to.

And so, with no recourse, I carried on, wondering "why" things were the way they were, and "why" we were required to follow this system that someone else (who we were never going to meet) made up as "the only way" to receive an education.

Now to be clear, I'm a learner. I always have been. There are very few things that don't interest me, even to this day, so I understand the value and opportunity in rounded learning. However, as an adult, I still dwell on that time period in my early life and recognize that there may be value found in an alternative education system that nurtures individual talents and interests in children, namely because I can see how many children with innate talents are not simply "slipping through the system" (as the media tries to sell you).

No. They are drowning in the system.

Aside from schools refusing to individualize paths, children are also discouraged from questioning nearly every aspect of the system they are in. And, as you have probably witnessed, pre-school young children are extremely fond of asking, "Why?"

"Why is the grass stuck to the ground?" "What are the stars made out of?" "Why is the ocean blue?"

The list goes on. But not for long if they are shut down one too many times.

From the beginning of "school" onward, we sadly discover that asking too many questions is met with an annoyed response from most teachers, authorities, and even parents. Why are things the way they are? Because they just are.

And because we are met with this continual response, we are subliminally programmed with the idea that to change these things for the better (perhaps), we will be embarking on an annoying (and potentially even dangerous) undertaking.

Differences in opinion - but especially differences that are alluded to in a pointed question format - are usually met with harsh opposition, even in adulthood.

I remember asking when I was 18 or 19 why we were still paying taxes, if the Boston Tea Party is so widely revered and supported … and was met with a strict lecture about the Unquestionable Thing That Cannot Be Changed and Why.

I still don't quite grasp that lecture or its foundation, as to me the solution to most individual and world problems and ideas for ultimate freedom can be found in my question … but that's for another book.

The root here is that if we are constantly "trained" not to ask too many questions, we are effectively breeding out the ability to create, to develop creative solutions, to bridge gaps between seemingly opposing problems and solutions, to innovate new systems, to integrate concepts into whole structures … and the list goes on.

Currently, children in public schools in the States are being taught that there is one way to solve a math problem to arrive at the correct answer, while the truth is that, depending upon the computing process of an individual's brain (and depending on the way that individual stores and accesses information), there are many ways to arrive at a correct answer.

And so, the question becomes, "Why are students being taught this way, especially when it limits some individual's potential?"

If we ponder for a moment, we'll arrive at the idea that kids cheat in school on tests all of the time, so educators need a unified way of preventing cheating, which has led to students being required to "show their work" of how they arrived at each math problem. If that work doesn't look like everyone else's work (and if the teacher isn't familiar with the method used), the student is pulled aside and explained that he must do it the way he was taught, and not in the way he was able to conceptualize the solution, even if it was correct. And we do this because a few bad apples were caught cheating on tests.

Why? What if this "solution" isn't the best solution? What if this solution teaches students that there is only one way of solving problems, and that if they can't solve one in a singular way, then there is no hope for one, so they should just give up? How does that impact a young adult's ability to navigate life? Does it make them more resilient? Adaptable? Or does it leave them stuck in a box the second they encounter a problem they can't immediately solve with the "only solution" they know?

There is one thing I want you to realize: "Why?" is the answer to every question.

Why? Because it is the root of the root. The direct pathway to foundational truth. The only taxi that will get you where you want to go, even when you're seemingly lost.

And, bonus: that taxi is free.

Asking "why?" in relation to all things, be it your personal reactions ("Why did I react that way?), others 'reactions ("Why did he or she behave that way?"), or systems of any kind, including belief systems ("Why do we do things/think this way? Why does something work this way?") is the ultimate catalyst for innovation.

Children ask "why?" so often because it is the most effective word-path to solid answers … and solutions.

"Why" is the question for every answer.

Why?

Because we must know the "why" of things before we can get to the next step: "What if?"

Don't Forget "What If?"

"Why are plates made the way that they are? What if they were different?"

This is a question I should have asked myself a long time ago, considering I eat off a plate every single day (talk about not seeing my eyelashes!).

Let's return to Mexico for a moment, where I'm sitting in a nonchalant dinner restaurant. I've just ordered the standard glass of vino and a starter when a pair of beautiful plates are laid on the table. They're very organic looking, with asymmetrical edges, and their color is a pleasing rust-tan. Almost clayware-like in appearance, their surface features a hint of rivulets running horizontally across to their edges, making them interesting to the hands and the eye. The waiter saw me looking and said casually that they were made by a local artist down the street, who uses pure cacao for the pigment, and rolls its fruit pod across each one to obtain the rivulets in the clay before drying.

My mouth fell open … because here was something that was so obvious (a plate), yet so innovative and sustainable and beautiful. Typically, we tend to feel lucky if we get one of those things (at an affordable price no less), yet this was all of those things in one.

I began to realize that every single thing we see every day has the potential to not only become a new invention that can fuel a business idea for us as individuals, but that these ideas can also put sustainability at the forefront of our daily lives by using natural materials in their production. All it takes is two simple questions to begin to see these possibilities: "Why?" and "What if?"

The lesson from that dinner?

No one thinks of changing their plate ... but if they did, they'd harness the potential to change the world.

The "Why" Exercise

I want you to ask yourself: "Why did I choose my career?"

Accept the immediate answer, whatever it is (i.e.: It was for the salary, the benefits, the space, etc …) then ask: "Why is that important to me?"

Try to get to specific answers here, such as, "It provides me financial freedom."

Write down your answer, then ask "Why is having/being financially free (insert your answer here) important to me?"

Once you get to the essence of what is important about your career (the above answer would be "security"), I want you to write it down. Then, I want you to ask yourself: "What was I passionate about as a child, or in college? Why?"

Repeat the same process here, then ask yourself: "Why did I give it up?"

You're going to run into your limiting beliefs surrounding your passion here, i.e.: the salary wasn't high enough (no financial freedom = no security), the prospects are limited, it's a dying art, ad infinitum.

Now, I want you to ask yourself why your passion can't provide you with financial freedom (security), a beautiful space, benefits, etc ...

What is it about your passion that limits it from being all of those things?

Perhaps it does not provide enough security because you are working for someone else. Can you start your passion yourself? Can you find a grant to help get you started?

And the magic question: what if you brought your passion online? How would that work?

For instance, I used to love the thought of being a professor (philosophy and psychology were the major options); however, the idea of working at a university day in and day out, without the financial security I needed, and with the oversight of certain limiting teaching systems, was a huge barrier to me following that passion.

So I decided to pivot. I wanted to teach, but I did not want the regulations of the school system limiting how I taught … and so I decided that I would teach via books and articles.

Is there a way you can follow your passion differently that will lead to what your career currently gives you (security, freedom, etc …)? You might need to do a little research, but I can almost guarantee there is a way. You just simply need to take your passion and run it through a list of questions:

- Why is my chosen field not as lucrative as I need it to be?

- How could it be made more lucrative? Can I combine it with something else?

- Can I offer this online?

- Can I make part of this a specialized niche?

- Why have other's failed in this passion? What can I do differently?

I'll give you another example to run with here. Remember my elementary school art adventures? Well, they carried over into middle and high school … but really started to dwindle in high school.

Why?

Because I had this belief that "art" as I thought of it (paintings and sketches) was a dying, well … art.

I had no idea "art" could be turned into illustration for, say, logos or branding, or could even be extremely lucrative online with a unique style. And so I gave it up.

Now, this isn't anyone's "fault" per say … but simply a matter of a lack of questioning on my part, and perhaps on my educator's part. Had I the foreknowledge, I could have asked myself the above questions, did a little research, and pivoted

100 percent to online illustration instead of dropping my passion.

What I want for you here is to get into the habit of asking the "why" and the "what if" of things now, so you never again miss an opportunity to take something you're interested in (even if it seems non-lucrative) and turn it into a unique idea, or career.

Chapter Two
Magical Thinking, Magical Linking

"Genius is finding the invisible link between things."- *Vladimir Nabokov*

For a moment, pretend you are an astrophysicist, or astronomer. You are looking up at the sky with the Big questions: "Why are we here? Who are we? And how can we ever know these answers?"

Of course, your goal in your field is to make some headway into answering these questions … so it's no surprise quite a bit of your life is going to be spent researching.

My question for you is: aside from what you learned at your university, where and what will you research from now on, to possibly answer these questions?

A common response would be that you will deepen your studies of physics (perhaps revisit the work of previous souls, namely geniuses, in the same field), quantum physics, multiverse theories, etc .. plus spend more time experimenting and looking up at the stars. In other words, all of your focus and energy will be spent devoted to the medium in which the Big answers may be found: physics.

Now, this is definitely necessary for any field, to be wholly immersed in the subject one is devoted to. However … I want to show you what happens when you dive down the rabbit hole of something else that appears to be completely unrelated to your focus.

Let's say you came across a statue of the Hindu God Shiva either at a museum, in a random book you happened to pick up, or at a decor shop. You may have a base knowledge of Hinduism, such as it being a monotheistic religion, cut with a good deal of pantheism, yet beyond that, you're essentially a dry sponge for Hinduism. In either scenario in which you stumbled upon Shiva, you'll likely get an explanation similar to:

> "Shiva (or Siva) is one of the most important gods in the Hindu pantheon and, along with Brahma and Vishnu, is considered a member of the holy trinity of Hinduism. He is associated with Time, and particularly as the destroyer of all things, as well as with creation. In Hinduism, the

universe is thought to regenerate in cycles (every 2,160,000,000 years). Shiva destroys the universe at the end of each cycle which then allows for a new Creation. He is the most important Hindu god for the Shaivism sect, the patron of Yogis and Brahmins, and also the protector of the Vedas, the sacred texts." [6]

While you might not be particularly religious, this idea of the creation and destruction of the universe within such a specific time frame intrigues you, and so you decide to look further into these mystical, "metaphorical" religious figures. Eventually, you stumble upon the Vedas and the Upanishads ... and the rabbit hole suddenly becomes a gold mine.

That is, at least, if you're Carl Sagan, world-renowned astrophysicist, leading consultant to NASA, holder of four degrees in physics, astronomy and astrophysics, Pulitzer-Prize winning author, and author of 20 books related to extraterrestrial life and the evolution of human intelligence.

Or, perhaps, if you're Neils Bohr, physicist and winner of the Nobel Prize in Physics who stated: "I go into the Upanishads to ask questions." [7]

Or maybe even if you're Robert Oppenheimer, the theoretical physicist who headed the lab that invented the first atom bomb (while not applauding such an invention in any way, you can see the relevance in relation to innovation), who remarked: "Access to the Vedas is the greatest privilege this century may claim over all previous centuries."

But the list of "big" names who dove down the rabbit hole of Hinduism's most sacred texts does not stop at physicists. Ralph Waldo Emerson, Rudolph Steiner, Henry David Thoreau, T.S. Eliot, Will Durant, Francois Voltaire, Steve Jobs, and Carl Jung, offer just a glimpse of the surface of an immense iceberg of figures in science, literature, philosophy, and technological development who upended the world and minds with their contributions.

Now, at first glance, would you link a Hindu deity ... to astrophysics?

Most of us wouldn't, unless we were given a reason to, or a hint as to why we would even want to be looking in that direction. And, even if we were interested in, say, ancient religions, we might feel like we're "wasting our time" deeply learning about them, since they're outside our current field.

I'm going to be blunt here: this is a majorly faulty thinking process. If anything can limit a human's potential and ability to innovate or succeed, it's lack of curiosity and suppression of curiosity.

How so?

In the business and university sphere, a technique referred to as cross-pollination is used among employees, students, and educators to help stimulate creative "ferments." In essence, individuals from different departments and disciplines are gathered together in order to create a knowledge-meld, in hopes of sparking and opening the minds of individuals through exposure to new ideas.

What does curiosity have to do with this?

I've observed that cross-pollination occurs naturally in individuals who exhibit high curiosity, not just of things in their immediate career "sphere," but also of a variety of seemingly unrelated things. As we saw earlier, curiosity regarding the Hindu religion and its deities (which seems lightyears away from being related to physics) ended up cross-pollinating with the half-flowered theories of physics waiting in Carl Sagan's, Neils Bohr's, and Robert Oppenheimer's minds.

As Nabokov put it, "Genius is finding the invisible link between things."

Cross-pollination makes it much more likely that such a link will be found between things, as your brain is wired to naturally compare past experiences with present circumstances. So, if you are heavily involved in physics, your brain will be subtly looking for similarities (even if they're metaphorical) in anything you study ... even Hinduism. And when a link is found in that unexpected place, it shifts the way you perceived everything you thought you "knew" about physics. It adds a dimension. A new layer. It explains what was previously an unexplainable concept, simply because it is using a different type of language: a religious language, rather than a scientific one. And because it is presented in this new format, new understanding may develop that can result in a larger theory, or invention.

Now, physics is a big field, and those were big examples ... but cross-pollination can be used on any level to generate new ideas, simply by making links between "things."

A form of cross-pollination (albeit small) naturally occurred when I saw the large vats of brewing herbs in my boyfriend's commercial kitchen as "giant teapots." From so many years of drinking tea, and then being exposed to something completely new, I was able to link (cross-pollinate) the idea of "tea" with what I was seeing in the brewing process, which then resulted in an entirely new process of creating the product that saved time and generated substantially more profit.

And the good news is, the more you practice making links between things, the easier and more habitual it becomes to do so.

I know time can become a factor here (as in not having enough free time every week to embark on tons of new experiences), which is why reading is your best friend.

But not just any type of reading: reading fiction.

This is for a very specific reason: our brains do not distinguish between fiction and reality when we're reading. The power of our imagination to completely consume our minds is awe-inspiring, and is illustrated in the following study [8]:

"Volunteers were asked to play a simple sequence of piano notes every day for five consecutive days. Their brains were scanned each day in the region connected to the finger muscles. Another set of volunteers were asked to imagine playing the notes instead, also having their brains scanned each day.

The top two rows in the image [scans] show the changes in the brain in those who played the notes. The middle two rows show the changes in those who simply imagined playing the notes. Compare this with the bottom two rows showing the brain regions of the control group, who didn't play nor imagine playing [the] piano.

You can clearly see that the changes in the brain in those who imaged playing piano are the same as in those who actually played piano. Really, your brain doesn't distinguish real from imaginary!" - *David R. Hamilton, PhD*

As you can see, your brain reacts to imagination and visualization as if you are experiencing reality. The great thing about reading fiction is that you can turn on an extremely high level of imagination and visualization for extended periods, and while imagining all types of experiences you may be "unable to" in reality.

In fiction, the main character(s) are viewed by your brain as "you" having the experience that the character is having, which is amazing news for trying out "new experiences"! You can read science fiction, mystery, travel mysteries (excellent for feeling as if you're delving into other cultures), you name it: your brain, as you, is going to experience it.

Of course, on this note, one of the other ideal ways to cross-pollinate is to travel, as much and as widely as you can. The exposure to new ideas, new faces, new art forms, new shapes, new smells, new everything, is unrivaled and relentless. This is one of the reasons you'll hear of many individuals (especially enlightened figures throughout history) returning from a sojourn with a paradigm-shifting idea or perspective - traveling makes it almost impossible not to.

If you're feeling stuck on your path, want to shift your life, generate a business idea, etc … I highly, highly recommend booking a ticket to somewhere that calls to you whose culture is completely different from your own.

Now, you don't have to go for a year and leave your life behind, but for just enough time to pull yourself out of everything you've ever known, so your mind can be pollinated with the nectar of diverse experience again … and bloom.

....

Magical Thinking, Magical Linking Exercise

Here, we are going to "play pretend" to help stretch your mind into a form of mental cross-pollination. Aside from getting curious and getting involved in activities and/or reading topics that are interesting to you, yet seemingly have nothing to do with your passion, career, etc ... I want you to try looking at things from different perspectives.

Imagine your idea, your passion, a situation, a problem (whichever you choose) and try looking at it like:

- A teacher

- A scientist

- A poet

- A criminal

- A child

- A grandparent

- A mime

Really delve into the thought process of a teacher, a scientist, a poet, etc ... and see what you come up with in how they would view and react to your idea, your situation, or your problem. This can mimic cross-pollination through a type of active empathy (imagining oneself in another's shoes), or what I call empathetic cross-pollination.

P.S.: If you already have an idea, this is an excellent tool to use to determine a marketing strategy. How do individual, niche audiences react to your idea?

Chapter One:

The Picking Up of Stones

What if your ceiling became your floor?

Legend has it that Siddhartha Gautama Buddha voraciously insisted that no statues be erected in his name.

"Make mirrors instead of statues," is a line often attributed to this figure we now see relentlessly ... in statue form around the world.

There is no actual account of the Buddha making this statement, but it does correspond to the fact that no bodily representations of the Buddha were made for roughly four of five centuries (the first are thought to have originated in the 1st of 2nd century due to Greek influence). Instead, artists took care to represent Buddha's teachings in other symbolic forms, such as the Lotus and the Wheel of the Dharma.

Buddha wasn't the only figure this idea surrounded. We see it in Christianity as well, as Jesus mentions in Leviticus 26:1, "You shall not make for yourselves idols ... nor shall you place a figured stone in your land to bow down to it ..."

Why was this occurring? After all, what could be the issue with erecting statues of a figure whose ideas illuminated minds and hearts around the world?

The key word lies in that exact question. " ... whose ideas illuminated minds and hearts around the world."

Now, I can't speak for Buddha or anyone else on the planet when I say this (and I'm probably going to strike an angry chord here in many people): the reason the erecting of statues is frowned upon is because the worshipping of figures that shared their knowledge is simply ... another heavy stone in your sack.

Admiring figures that radically shifted the world with their information is noble. Worshipping those figures is the equivalent of believing their abilities are unattainable for yourself. In my opinion, erecting statues of Buddha was avoided for so many centuries because it was a way to encourage followers to place their attention and love on the teachings, not the teacher.

Why?

Because the information that Jesus, Buddha, and other enlightened figures shared with the world is accessible to everyone. And, in the same way, the "ideas" and "innovations" brought forth by "geniuses" and "gurus" is also accessible to everyone.

The only difference between "us" and the geniuses of the world comes down to curiosity (willingness to learn), receptibility (the ability to be open to new ideas), and unshakeable belief and courage (which gives us persistence to follow through).

The danger of worshipping others who are sharing or have shared valuable ideas and innovations with the world is that we become programmed with the subconscious belief that they "have something" that we do not (or cannot) have. And this belief, in turn, makes us feel like we have to find that grand "thing" before we can start creating.

In addition, we run the risk of trying to be just like those figures that we worship, to the point where we miss out on information that is waiting specifically for us. We put on blinders to our soul, our creativity, and our unique way of seeing, by trying to see like someone else.

And finally, worshipping figures in any field trains your brain not to look for information yourself, to make your own unique links, or to search for answers yourself, but to simply wait for someone else to tell you" how it should be done." Waiting for idols to provide information without seeking information for yourself is a one-way road that is a dead end for creativity and authenticity.

Again, this is not to say we can't admire figures that shared amazing information with us (heck, I have to continuously remind myself not to erect a statue of Kahlil Gibran every time I read a single paragraph of one of his stories), it simply means that these figures we giving you information that is accessible to all of us.

And they knew it.

I'm going to dive into some personal spirituality here for context. Why do I claim this information is available to all of us? Because in my mind and heart, information is another word for Source, Spirit, or God, or whatever name you have for "it." Jesus admonished idol worship because of the idea that there is only one God. One source of all information in the universe. Buddha also recognized this idea by putting emphasis on the Path and Dharma (the ultimate information), rather than himself.

For me, recognizing that all humans, including myself and you, are capable of becoming the next Buddha or Jesus or President or Steve Jobs or whatever idolized person you want to insert here removes a barrier to creation that would exist if I worshipped these figures as greater than my own potential as a human. I admire these figures, and acknowledge that I have some work to do before I can claim to be "just as enlightened, technologically savvy, charismatic, etc ..." as them ... but I don't discount the possibility that if I applied myself, with all of the information provided by life and Source itself, I could become similar to them one day, in the same way that I know you could as well.

Recognizing that there is one source of information to worship (whether you want to call it God or the binary-coded universe) removes the barrier to entry we place on ourselves to be like "famous" figures, because we realize we have the same potential as those people we once worshipped. Because they are just that: people.

My favorite way to condense this?

Set down the stones of worship, pick up the stones of admiration and curiosity, and realize, "You are the guru." You have the same amount of potential that any other human on this earth has. Depending on your circumstances, you may have to look in different places, but once you begin the search, you will not be let down.

....

Picking Up The Stones Excercise

The entire idea behind "setting down your stones" in the earlier chapters of this book was to help you become a vessel for new ideas. After all, a cup that is half-full cannot be filled with as much new water.

Or, as I like to put it, I wanted you to reach a point where you agreed to set down your stones of past programming and beliefs, so that when someone asked you, "Is your cup half empty or half full?" you answered:

"My cup is so empty that it's overflowing with possibility."

However, I never intended for you to never have any stones. The key lies in how you position the ones you do have.

Do you carry them on your back, so that you are weighed down with set ideas of "how things are"? Do you carry half of them in front of you, so that your load is easier to carry ... but that you're constantly unable to see new, valuable concepts waiting right in front of you?

Or, do you place them underneath you? Do you pick them up and then use them to build a foundation of knowledge, opposing concepts, and diverse experiences and viewpoints that cross-pollinate your sponge?

Do you take the stones of your past, look at them and ask, "These preconceived notions may have once limited my perception and growth, but now they are valuable tools of reference to compare the past with the future. Do they have a place in my foundation?"

Do you pick up the stones of your present and future, inscribed with curiosity, determination, and a new way to think, and set them down beside the stones of your past, so you can always draw knowledge from both?

When you have done these things, and let your imagination run wild with ideas and possibilities in previous chapters … it is now time to take this foundation, and bring an idea into the world.

In previous chapters, I encouraged you to not censor your ideas, no matter how outlandish they may be (to, in a sense, try not to slow down your fall down rabbit holes). I encouraged you only to make links with abandon, and dream without barriers or preconceived notions.

Now, the next step begins. How can you bring your idea to life?

This is the step that is actually the most challenging, and it's the reason I encouraged you to not think much of it until now. "Figuring out" how you are going to create something in the "real world" often puts out the fire of creativity before it even starts providing warmth.

Ironically, the same process that got you to your idea is going to get it off the ground.

A first dip into this pool is to consider your audience: who would benefit the most from your idea? I like to use the exercise from the previous chapter Magical Thinking, Magical Linking in order to glean different audience perspectives and how each would use and/or think about your idea. This is also useful when it comes time for marketing, or even if you need to apply for grants or funding.

If you haven't asked the question yet, "Can I bring my idea online?" definitely ask it now. Even if it seems more like a brick and mortar business, trust me: there are ways to start doing what you love now even if you can't afford to invest fully right now.

For example: Let's say you would love to have a huge farm on many acres, where you sell produce to the public. Maybe you even want a restaurant or store on the farm. You know how to grow things well, have plenty of practice knowing which plants pollinate together, and have perhaps even taken a class on permaculture.

Yet there's one problem: you can't afford to purchase a huge farm right now.

Most people would drop the dream right here. But others will pivot in never-thought-of-directions.

I walked past a small advertisement on a window the other day which read: "Do you want to grow your own food, but don't know how to start a garden? We can help!" The ad then went on to say a few lines about how they help design fruit and vegetable gardens (all sizes) for people at their homes … taking the guesswork out for those wanting to grow their own food!

The magic of this idea? How many articles and books have you seen online about "how to start your own garden"? Probably hundreds.

This idea gives people the opportunity to have someone else help them get started on a garden, even if it's just a small one, so they can be sure to get it right and actually make it fruitful.

And the best part about this? Whoever thought of this idea may not be able to afford their own farm to sell veggies … but they can still practice (while perfecting) their passion with an extremely lucrative, similar business idea, which will eventually provide them with funds for a down payment on farm land.

They key with getting your idea into the world? Creativity and curiosity. How can you bring this passion to life, in a different way? What unique problem can it solve with just a few tweaks to its selling structure?

This is another reason why it is so important to cross-pollinate your life, because you end up seeing different ways of doing similar things. You break the mold of not only the big concepts, but the smaller, structural ones as well (farm vs. mobile, individualized farming). If you were only exposed to traditional farmers day in and day out, you may think that having a farm is the only way of realizing your dream of harvesting food.

Also, consider ways to subset your passion and bring it online. Perhaps your real passion regarding farming is figuring out how to structure the land and layer the plants in order to produce the most efficient yield (aka: permaculture). You could theoretically sell and online course on permaculture (Udemy is a favorite) and find real pleasure in what you're doing, while making an income, and preparing for an expanded future in farming.

Always consider: what aspect of your passion does your audience want or need? And how can you give it to them in a better, more efficient, more unique way than it is currently being offered? Ask questions about the niche. Interview people. Ask their opinion on things related to your idea.

Another good way to start generating ideas related to how you will bring this thing to life is to think of something within your niche or passion that makes you angry or annoyed. Focus on that, and what you could possibly do to improve it so that it no longer bothers you. Chances are, someone else can benefit from the solution you just provided. (i.e.: many people may be annoyed at not knowing where to start with their gardens. You came to the rescue.)

The foundation is here. Stone by stone, your idea is waiting to be erected into life. The most important thing is that you don't let societal structure limit your ideas. That you become so ecstatic about what you want that you find a creative way to pull it out into the light. Don't be afraid to break boundaries, turn things upside down, and think magically, straddling the edge of limitations so that you can see beyond them while also working with them. Limitations are, after all, here to provide structural foundations to ideas so that they can be made tangible in this reality.

It is our job, as creators, to lasso our dreams floating in the sky, wrestle them to earth, dive with them down a rabbit hole ... and emerge with the magic-infused tools to build our house of passion.

Introduction

At the beginning of this book, you were an "ending." An adult with an education by society ... and a heavy sack of stones.

I spoke about Mandarin Chinese, and how sentences are structured with the past coming before the future, in order to illustrate its influence on future events.

Because of this, I want you to look back on yourself. On the "you" that was an "ending" at the beginning of this book. I want you to remember what "you" felt as that end result of years of various programs within society telling you how to "think" (conform) and what was possible for you.

I want you to do this so that when you feel like giving up on this new beginning (you right now), you will look beside you and see your past self. And it will remind you that if you give up on this dream ... you will become that past self again, and perhaps until the end of this life.

I also mentioned in your past that the ending of a book should never be an ending.

It should be a beginning. Your Beginning. A place where worded ideas from me cease, and your use of them in the world commences.

So with that, I will step aside … and allow you to introduce your new idea. Your forgotten passion. Your dream-become-manifest.

Your new life.

References:

1. Yan Gu, Yeqiu Zheng, and Marc Swerts. "Which Is in Front of Chinese People, Past or Future? The Effect of Language and Culture on Temporal Gestures and Spatial Conceptions of Time." Cognitive Science. Vol. 43, Issue 12.

2. Martin Maier and Rasha Abdel Rahman. Native Language Promotes Access to Visual Consciousness. Association for Psychological Science. Sage Journals. Vol. 29, Issue 11. 2018.

3. Thomas M. Bartol Jr, Cailey Bromer, Justin Kinney, Michael A. Chirillo, Jennifer N. Bourne, Kristen M. Harris, Terrence J. Sejnowski. Nanoconnectomic upper bound on the variability of synaptic plasticity. Elife. DOI: 10.7554/eLife.10778. 2015.

4. Robert F. Service. "DNA Could Store All Of The World's Data In One Room." Science Magazine. 2017.

5. World History Encyclopedia. Shiva.

6. Viraj Kulkarni. "What Erwin Schrödinger Said About the Upanishads." Science The Wire. 2020.

7. David R. Hamilton. "Does Your Brain Distinguish Real From Imaginary?" Dr.DavidHamilton.com. 2014.